Lexi Re...

Art...

BElieve IN YOUrself

Fun mindfulness activities and tools you can use every day!

Published in Great Britain
By Outset Publishing Ltd

First edition published June 2021

Written by Lexi Rees and Sasha Mullen
Illustration and Design by Eveyjoan

ISBN: 978-1-913799-06-9

www.lexirees.co.uk
www.themindfulmentors.com

IT'S OFFICIAL, YOU ARE AMAZING!

Everybody has moments when they don't feel amazing inside. We might be sad or angry or frustrated, or there could even be lots of emotions all jumbled up inside us. It can be difficult when this happens, but the good news is there are lots of things we can do to help our minds process these emotions.

Through this journal, you're going to build your very own mindfulness <u>tool kit</u>. Every chapter you complete unlocks awesome new skills. By the time you finish all the activities, you'll know how to do all these things:

- Believe in yourself
- Be more confident
- Concentrate better
- Boost your memory
- Be aware of how you feel
- Understand how others might feel
- Discover your happy self

Look out for this icon as you go through the book.

With these tools, you can be your most amazing self every day.

How To Use This Journal

The journal is divided into sections. Each section builds a set of skills through several different activities. Just like you might train for a sport or learn how to play a musical instrument, the activities in each section are designed to help you practise these skills so you can get really good at them.

You can work through most of the sections in order or, if there are areas that are worrying you at the moment, you might like to turn to those sections and start there.

By practising mindfulness and building your tool kit, you can take control of your mind and body.

BE YOU, Believe in Yourself!

Activity Key

- Science
- Art
- Visualisation
- Game
- Analysis
- To do
- Breathing

Keep an eye out for these tips throughout this journal!

MINDFUL MAGIC

When you use this tool kit, you're practising "mindfulness". Mindfulness helps you to accept things as they are. There's no judgement or criticism, just understanding.

CONTENTS

This journal belongs to:

. . . .

Chapter 1

Recognise Your Strengths

In this chapter we're going to:

- Acknowledge **you** are amazing

- Celebrate **your** achievements

- Discover how **your** breathing can help **you** feel stronger

Check in with yourself, how do you feel right now?

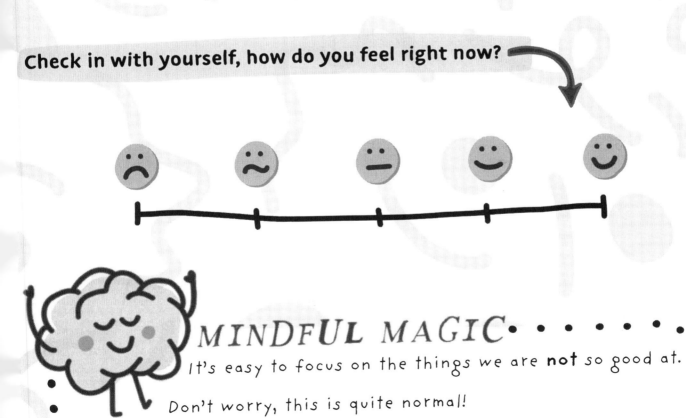

MINDFUL MAGIC

It's easy to focus on the things we are **not** so good at.

Don't worry, this is quite normal!

BRAIN SCIENCE

The **prefrontal cortex** is the part of the brain that controls muscles, so it's the part that's used if we're doing things like learning to walk or dance. It also helps us to learn new skills like solving challenging maths problems or playing the piano.

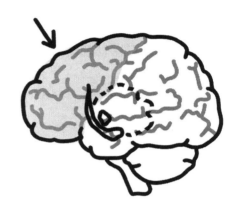

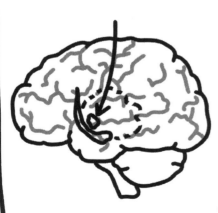

The **amygdala** part of the brain is only about the size of an almond. It makes us aware of our feelings and defines how we react to situations. For example, if you are about to perform in front of the whole school and parents - it will fire up and either make you unable to speak, help you strut onto stage confidently, or persuade you to run out of the room!

The **hippocampus** part of the brain stores our short term and long-term memory, like a USB stick. For example, if you've just done fractions in maths class and you have to do a page of sums for homework, your hippocampus will help you to remember how fractions work.

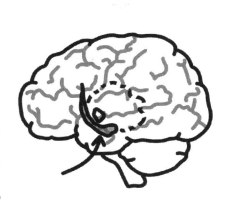

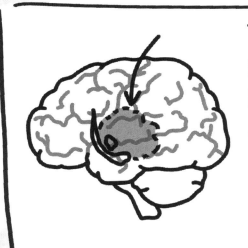

The **insula** is the part of the brain that provides empathy and helps you understand both your own feelings and other people's feelings. For example, if you hurt your friend's feelings by not playing with them, the insula kicks in so you can react sympathetically.

MINDFUL MAGIC

We're going to learn more about how the brain works, and how to train it, as we go through this book.

Colour in the different parts of the brain

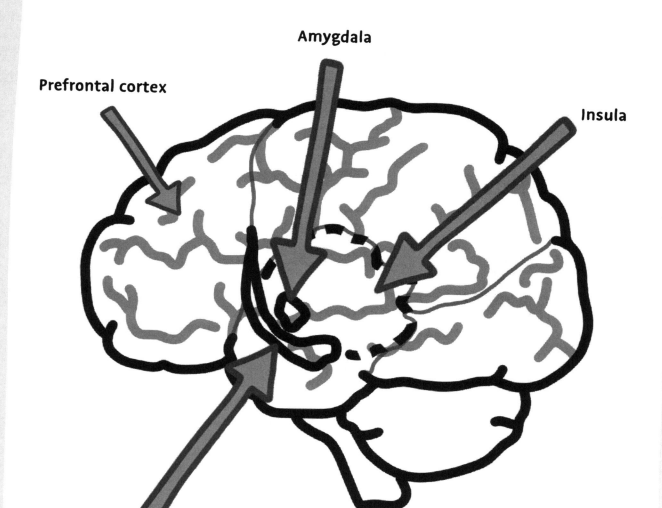

Amygdala

Prefrontal cortex

Insula

Hippocampus

Shine like the sun

Marvellous Me Potion

How many ingredients can **you** add to the potion?
Think about...

- **Things I'm good at:** Are you brilliant at listening? Or solving problems? Or riding your bike?

- **Things about me:** Are you friendly? Funny? Clever? Sporty? Quiet? Chatty?

- **Things I have:** A best friend? A big smile? A pet? A favourite toy? A nice teacher?

Cut your potion out and stick it up on the wall! You can add other things to the potion when you think of them.

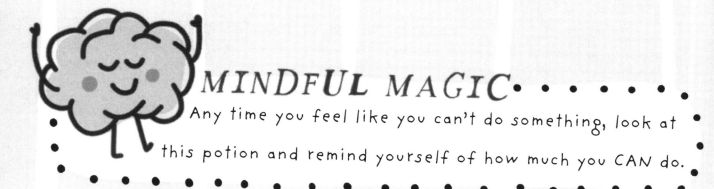

MINDFUL MAGIC

Any time you feel like you can't do something, look at this potion and remind yourself of how much you CAN do.

Marvellous Me

I am good at:

I am:

I have:

This page is blank to allow for awesome
potion making on the other side!

Wordsearch

Sometimes things may be hidden, but if we know where to look, they are always there!

C	Y	C	K	W	M	S	C	E	N	P	N	L	I	R
O	E	R	D	V	Y	U	C	I	O	O	P	Y	E	A
N	S	P	V	N	T	I	A	S	F	R	Z	L	T	O
C	Y	G	S	G	T	R	I	E	H	T	A	E	R	B
E	S	E	N	C	B	T	W	W	M	X	L	W	D	A
N	D	T	A	I	I	S	S	E	N	L	L	I	T	S
T	H	R	R	V	L	M	K	F	U	U	A	A	Q	R
R	P	A	I	E	G	E	Q	B	E	F	E	C	U	E
A	E	T	P	C	N	D	E	L	M	E	R	N	I	V
T	Y	V	U	P	C	G	Y	F	O	C	A	N	E	Y
E	F	Z	E	N	Y	D	T	Q	T	A	W	N	T	D
Y	J	N	C	I	P	Z	C	H	I	E	A	E	B	U
T	H	O	U	G	H	T	S	P	O	P	B	Z	E	S
N	R	A	E	L	E	C	R	P	N	X	O	R	H	C
H	X	Q	D	I	S	U	A	G	S	F	O	C	U	S

ACHIEVE

AWARE

BRAIN

BREATHE

CALM

CONCENTRATE

EMOTIONS

FEELINGS

FOCUS

HAPPY

LEARN

PEACEFUL

POSITIVITY

PRACTICE

QUIET

RELAX

STILLNESS

STRENGTH

THOUGHTS

ZEN

All About Me

This is me!

When you're aware of your strengths and the areas you need to work on, your mind is better prepared to tackle things you find tricky.

Things I find easy are:

How did you become so MARVELLOUS at these things?

Practising   Concentrating   Dedication   Being Calm   Being Brave

Use a Goal Tracker

Can you think of 4 things you would like to get better at?

1.

2.

3.

4.

Each week, pick one thing and decide what the best way to improve at it would be. Try to do it every day for a week.

Use the goal tracker on the next pages to keep a record of your progress.

MY GOAL TRACKER

Week 1

This week I am focusing on: ....

MONDAY

TUESDAY

To get better at it,
I am going to:

☐ Practise
☐ Concentrate
☐ Persevere
☐ Stay calm
☐ Be brave

WEDNESDAY

THURSDAY

FRIDAY

SATURDAY

SUNDAY

MY GOAL TRACKER

Week 2

This week I am focusing on: . . . .

MONDAY

TUESDAY

To get better at it, I am going to:

☐ Practise
☐ Concentrate
☐ Persevere
☐ Stay calm
☐ Be brave

WEDNESDAY

THURSDAY

FRIDAY

SATURDAY

SUNDAY

MY GOAL TRACKER

Week 3

This week I am focusing on: ....

MONDAY

TUESDAY

To get better at it,
I am going to:

- ☐ Practise
- ☐ Concentrate
- ☐ Persevere
- ☐ Stay calm
- ☐ Be brave

WEDNESDAY

THURSDAY

FRIDAY

SATURDAY

SUNDAY

MY GOAL TRACKER

Week 4

This week I am focusing on: . . . .

MONDAY

TUESDAY

To get better at it,
I am going to:

- [ ] Practise
- [ ] Concentrate
- [ ] Persevere
- [ ] Stay calm
- [ ] Be brave

WEDNESDAY

THURSDAY

FRIDAY

SATURDAY

SUNDAY

Fingertip Breathing

Pick a strength statement from below.

Say one word from your chosen statement as you fold each finger down.

As you breathe out, open your hand. Repeat this as many times as you want.

I am my best self

I am calm and happy

I am brave and strong

MINDFUL MAGIC • • • • •

If there are other people around and you don't want to say it out loud, you can whisper it very quietly, or write it down.

Congratulations!

You have unlocked your first three mindfulness tools! These will help you to see yourself in a positive light.

In the Toolbox:

 Check your Marvellous Me potion every morning to remind yourself how amazing you are.

 Use the Goal Tracker to celebrate your achievements!

Make a Fingertip Breathing strength statement.

You are now ready to use these tools anywhere!

Chapter 2

Zen Your Space

In this chapter we're going to:

- Be aware of how you feel
- Turn negative thoughts into positives ones
- Find your calm and happy place

Before we start, how are you feeling right now?

I'm feeling: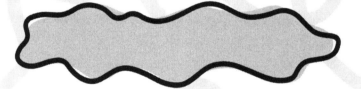

Lots of people find it helpful to say it out loud. Give it a try. Take a deep breath and read what you have written.

MINDFUL MAGIC

It can be difficult to acknowledge our feelings and even harder to say them out loud, maybe because we're worried what people might think of us, especially if our feeling is a negative emotion. Don't worry, this is quite normal!

Label the different parts of the brain:

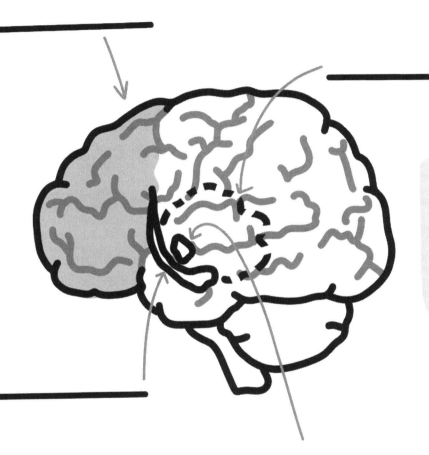

KEY
- Prefrontal cortex
- Amygdala
- Hippocampus
- Insula

All of these parts of the brain work together when you are practising mindfulness.

MINDFUL MAGIC

Understanding the different functions of your brain helps you to notice when one part is active.

Doodle Time

Pick a colour pencil that matches how you are feeling at the moment. Begin by making a mark anywhere on the page and then see where the pencil takes you.

Maybe you'll find that you draw why you are feeling that way, maybe you'll draw a range of patterns, or just cover the paper with your coloured emotion. There is no right or wrong answer, just let the colour flow onto the paper.

FRAME IT!

Think of a time when you felt calm and happy. Draw it here.

Use this memory to support you when you are feeling any negative emotions.

1. Close your eyes
2. Focus on the moment in this picture
3. Take a breath in and smile
4. Breathe out and feel yourself in that calm/ happy place
5. Slowly open your eyes and bring yourself back into the present

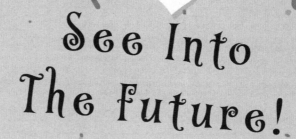

See Into The Future!

How to make your fortune teller:

1. Carefully cut out the big square on the next page.
2. Fold it in half vertically and press the crease, then open it flat again.
3. Fold it in half horizontally and press the crease, then open it flat again.
4. Turn it over so you can't see the writing and put it on a table.
5. Fold the four corners in so they meet in the middle.
6. Turn it over and fold the four new corners into the middle. Turn it over again.
7. Wriggle your thumbs and two fingers into the little pockets and pinch them together. You should now have the four pictures on top.

How to use your fortune teller:

1. Choose one of the four pictures.
2. Spell out the word, opening or closing the fortune teller for each letter.
3. Look inside and pick one of the numbers you can see.
4. Count to that number, opening and closing the fortune teller as you go.
5. Look inside again and pick a number.
6. Open that number to reveal your fortune!

*Of course, we can't really see into the future... Mindfulness is about being present and not worrying about the past or the future. See if you can forget your worries and have a laugh in the present.

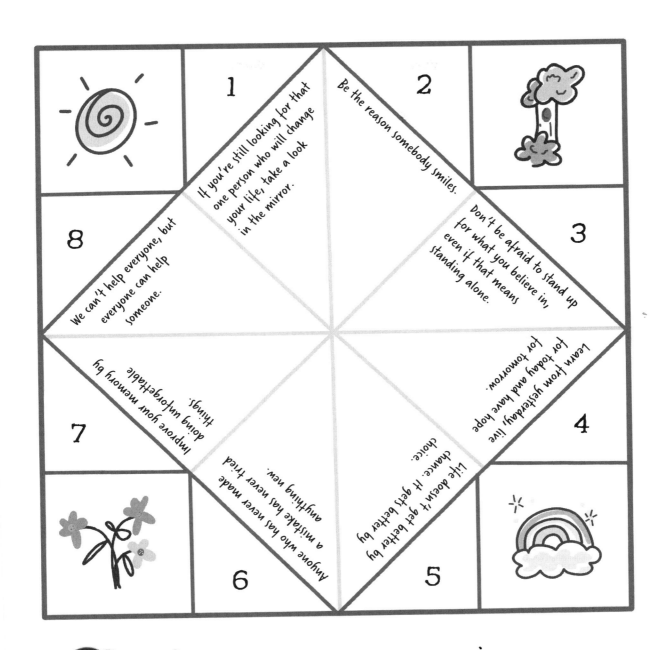

1

2

8

3

7

4

6

5

If you're still looking for that one person who will change your life, take a look in the mirror.

Be the reason somebody smiles.

We can't help everyone, but everyone can help someone.

Don't be afraid to stand up for what you believe in, even if that means standing alone.

Learn from yesterday, live for today and have hope for tomorrow.

Improve your memory by doing unforgettable things.

Anyone who has never made a mistake has never tried anything new.

Life doesn't get better by chance. It gets better by choice.

MINDFUL MAGIC
Even if you are laughing and chatting while doing this activity, you are still practising mindfulness. You don't need to be sitting still or quietly. Just be aware of your emotions.

This page is blank so you can
cut out your fortune teller.

MY Zen Zone

when do you feel calm?

what are you doing at the time?

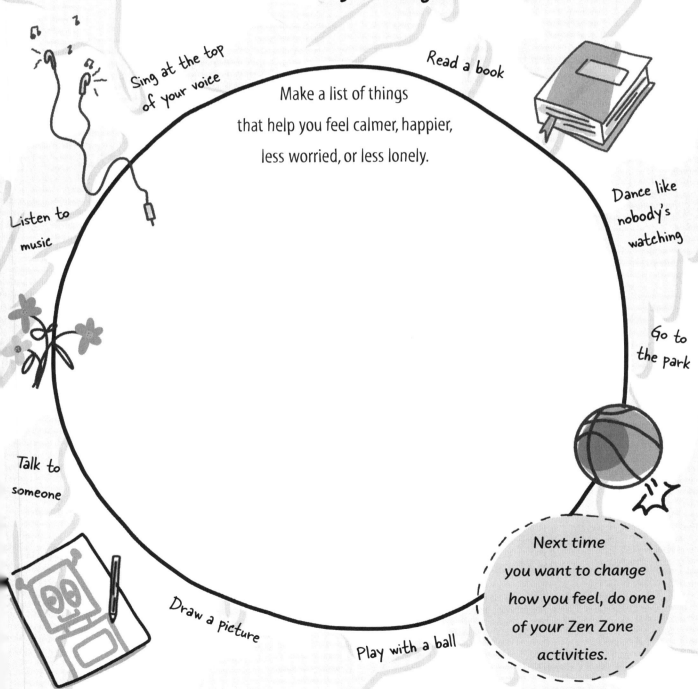

Make a list of things
that help you feel calmer, happier,
less worried, or less lonely.

Sing at the top
of your voice

Read a book

Listen to
music

Dance like
nobody's
watching

Go to
the park

Talk to
someone

Draw a Picture

Play with a ball

Next time
you want to change
how you feel, do one
of your Zen Zone
activities.

Lava Lamp

To make your lava lamp you will need:

- A large clear glass jar or bottle
- Water
- Vegetable oil (or baby oil)
- Alka Seltzer
- Liquid food colouring

Alternative: Swap the food colouring for glow in the dark pigment (photo luminescent pigment).

Instructions

1. Fill the jar with water to about 1/4 full.
2. Add enough vegetable oil to almost fill the bottle, leaving about an inch at the top.
3. Next, add a few drops of food colouring.
4. Now it's time for the magic! Add a teaspoon of Alka Seltzer (if yours are in tablet form, break the tablets into quarters and add a quarter tablet). Leave the lid off.
5. Watch the lava lamp come to life with bubbles!
6. After a few minutes the reaction will settle down.
7. To start it again, simply add more Alka Seltzer.

You can store the container and use it at a later time. If you want to put a lid on the container, make sure the reaction has completely stopped, as gas can build up and cause the container to explode.

Draw or stick a photo of your lava lamp here!

Tense and Release

Start by finding a quiet space

Stand up tall, feet shoulder width apart, and let your arms relax down by your side.

Take three deep breaths in through your nose and out through your mouth.

Notice your chest and tummy rising and falling as you breathe.

Close your eyes and clear your mind.

Open your eyes and be aware of your surroundings.

Breathe in and squeeeeeeeeeeeze your fists - feel the tension fill your whole body.

Relax your body.

Relax your hands.

Breathe out and release your fists – feel the tension flow from your whole body. Let all your negative emotions wash away with it.

MINDFUL MAGIC

You may need to repeat this more than once to feel the calming effects.

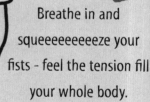

Congratulations!

You have unlocked your next three mindfulness tools! These help you to recognise any negative feelings and allow yourself to be happier.

In the Toolbox:

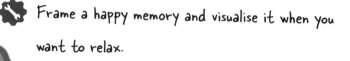 Frame a happy memory and visualise it when you want to relax.

Do an activity that takes you to your Zen Zone when you want to change how you feel.

Use the Tense and Release breathing technique to squeeze away any worries.

You are now ready to use these tools anywhere!

Chapter 3

Master Your Mind

In this chapter we're going to:

- Understand how **your mind and body** react to things

- Notice when **your mind wanders**

- Be more aware of **your surroundings**

Before we start, check in with yourself.

What are you thinking about right now? School work, completing your computer game, food, being told off, your birthday party...

My mind is thinking about:

Imagine you're about to meet a huge celebrity. Your heart may start beating faster. This is your body sending a message to your brain that you are excited.

Becoming more aware of body sensations will help your brain to read and understand the messages sent by your body faster.

MINDFUL MAGIC

You may notice a difference between what your body is feeling and what your mind is thinking. This is OK, we rely on our bodies to send messages to our minds, and sometimes our mind can take a little while to read the message.

The Tremendous Triangle

Who we are reflects our thoughts, plus our actions, plus our feelings.

Your thoughts affect your
actions and feelings

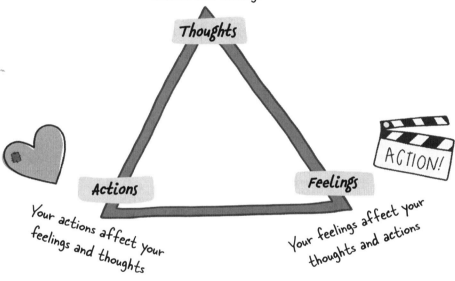

Thoughts

Actions

Feelings

Your actions affect your
feelings and thoughts

Your feelings affect your
thoughts and actions

"The world we have created is a product of our thinking; it cannot be changed without changing our thinking." – Albert Einstein

MINDFUL MAGIC

Did you know your body is like an unconscious mind? That means it can't tell the difference between an actual experience and a thought! So, if you train your mind to replace negative thoughts with positive ones, your body will behave differently.

Let It Go

If someone upsets you, there's no point holding onto emotions that cause you pain and upset.

Begin by acknowledging your emotion.

Then breathe in and out slowly FIVE times:

...five
four
three
two
one...

Now write down what you would want to say to the person that has made you unhappy, and what they might say back.

MIND MAZE

Start here

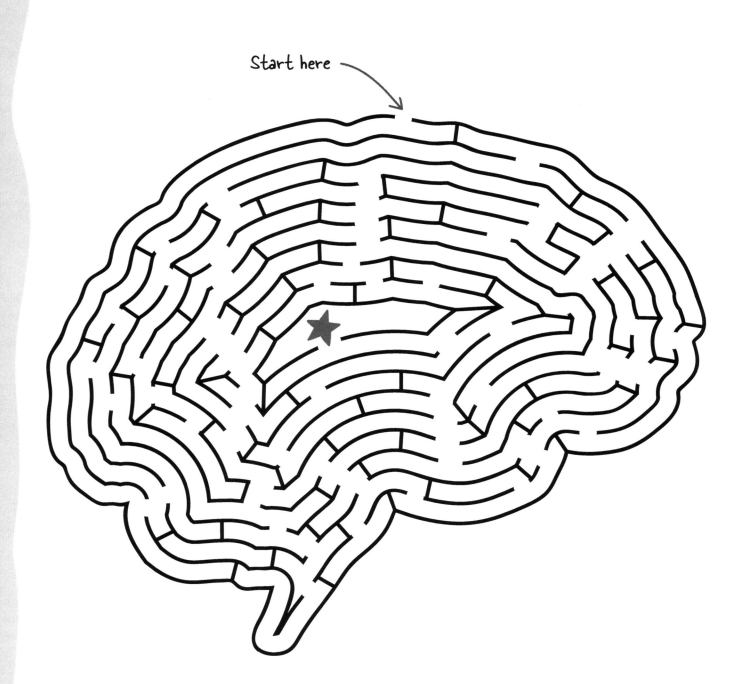

TRAVELLING THOUGHTS

Did you know that over **60,000 thoughts** go through our mind every day? Some thoughts are exactly the same as yesterday, others are about the future. Very few thoughts are actually about what you are doing at the present moment.

Try this exercise and see how many times your mind wanders. If your mind wanders, just accept it, then bring your attention back to your body.

- Make yourself comfortable, sitting or lying down.
- Close your eyes and relax.
- Notice your breathing. In and out. In and out.
- Let go of any tension in your body.
- Imagine your breath flowing all the way down to your toes.
- Now think about your legs. How do they feel?
- Relax your whole body.
- Notice your tummy and chest expanding and shrinking as you breathe in and out.
- Move your attention to your arms and shoulders. Let them go floppy.
- Soften your face. Is your jaw tight or relaxed? Are your eyebrows furrowed?
- Bring your attention back to your breath, following the in and out movement.
- Now open your eyes.

This can be an activity for two or more. You can ask a parent or friend to read you the script.

What thoughts popped into your mind while you were doing that exercise?

MINDFUL MAGIC

Everybody's mind wanders sometimes, it's quite natural. By practising mindfulness, you're training yourself to bring your attention back to whatever you should be doing. This could be your homework, a science experiment, watching TV, a conversation, or just what you're eating.

Transfiguration

Whatever the situation, changing just one thing can give you a different outcome. Here is an example:

Thought:
My friend won't play with me

Feeling:
This makes me feel sad

Inaction:
I sit on my own at lunchtime and have no one to talk to

But, I can make myself feel better by taking action

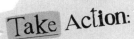
Take Action:

I can ask someone else to play with me
or
I can do something different
or
I can tell my friend how that makes me feel

Now it's your turn to
TRANSFIGURE A WORRY...

I am worrying about...

....

....

....

Oo●

But, I can make myself feel better by taking action

I could do these 3 things:

1.

2.

3.

MINDFUL MAGIC • • • • •
This is a really powerful tool, but can take a bit of practice to get used to. Next time something is upsetting you, give it a try!

A Mirror to Your Mind!

Method:

1. Fold your mirrored card into three long sections. Each segment must be the same diameter as the tube (about 4 cm wide). Cut off any excess.

2. Sticky tape the long sides together to form a triangular prism.

3. Push the prism into the kitchen roll tube.

4. Make two plastic circles by drawing around the tube. One needs to fit snugly inside the tube, so you will need to trim this very slightly. The other will sit outside.

You Will Need:

- An empty cardboard tube, about 20cm long e.g. an empty kitchen roll or section of a wrapping paper roll
- A4 sized mirrored card, about 1cm shorter than the tube
- Small colourful objects – sequins/ tiny beads/ pieces of sweet wrappers
- Two plastic circles e.g. cut from a clean recycled plastic container
- One cardboard circle
- Scissors
- Glue stick
- Sticky tape
- Materials to decorate the outside e.g. recycled paper, stickers, glitter etc.

If you don't have mirrored card, you can either stick metallic tape or smooth tinfoil onto both sides of a piece of card.

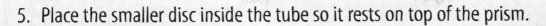

5. Place the smaller disc inside the tube so it rests on top of the prism.

6. Pour the beads/sequins into the end of the tube on top of the plastic disc. Don't overfill it, they need to move around.

7. Place the other plastic disc onto the end of the tube on the outside and tape into place. Don't worry if the tape is visible – you'll cover it up when you decorate the tube.

8. Turn the kaleidoscope round so you have the other end facing you.

9. Make a peephole in the middle of the cardboard circle.

10. Tape the cardboard circle to the end of the tube.

11. Decorate the outside of the tube.

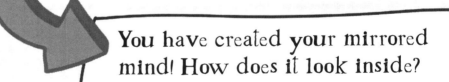

You have created your mirrored mind! How does it look inside?

_____

_____

_____

MINDFUL MAGIC

Try using this kaleidoscope when your mind is racing. Focus on the shapes and patterns. Let them settle and pay attention to your breathing.

❄ Snow Angels

1. Find a comfortable place and lie down on your back.
2. Spread your arms, palms facing down and feet as wide as you can.
3. Take a deep breath in and out through your nose.
4. Take another breath in, and let it out through your mouth.
5. Begin to slide your arms and legs up and down along the floor, following the rhythm of your breathing.
6. Try moving your arms and legs faster a few times.
7. Bring your movement back to the rhythm of your breathing.
8. Finish by placing your arms by your legs and lie in a pencil position.

How did that exercise make you feel?

_____

What thoughts popped into your head while you were doing it?

_____

How do you feel now?

_____

MINDFUL MAGIC

When you feel dark and stormy, movement can distract the mind from those negative thoughts and feelings.

Congratulations!

You have unlocked another three mindfulness tools! These help you to spot when your mind wanders and become more focused.

In the Toolbox:

 Catch any sneaky Travelling Thoughts by scanning your body.

 Use Transfiguration to change the outcome of situations.

Let a Snow Angel calm your mind.

You are now ready to use these tools anywhere!

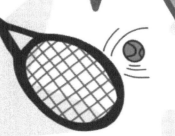

Chapter 4

In this chapter we're going to:

- Recognise that a busy mind is normal

- Discover your distraction danger zones

- Learn how to organise your thoughts

Before we start, check in with yourself.

How are you feeling? What animal would represent this feeling? Here are some ideas, or you can make up your own.

Lazy Lizard

Mad Monkey

Grizzly Bear

Talkative Toucan

The first step to being self-aware is noticing how we are feeling in ourselves. It can be easier to spot this through the characteristics of an animal.

MINDFUL MAGIC • • • • • • •
Just like the colour of a chameleon, our feelings will change.

Grow Your Brain

Practising mindfulness can actually help GROW your brain! The brain is a muscle so, like a body builder doing weight training at the gym, you can make it bigger and stronger. That means you can train it to get better at noticing things, paying attention, and focusing on tasks for longer.

Put your existing skills into the right boxes and see how you can begin training your brain every day, without even thinking about it.

My Prefrontal Cortex
What can you do? E.g. play football, speak a foreign language, ice skate

My Insula
What emotions can you recognise?
E.g. kindness, frustration, anger, sadness, excitement, loneliness

My Amygdala
E.g. public speaking, making mistakes, getting lost, being lonely

My Hippocampus
What are you good at remembering?
E.g. jokes, song lyrics, science formulae, times tables, bus routes, shopping lists

Mischievous Monkeys

Picture a monkey. What is it thinking?

With over 60,000 thoughts every day, your mind is busier than a whole troop of monkeys. This can make it difficult to focus.

MINDFUL MAGIC
Once you've noticed your "monkey mind", you can train it to focus.

SPOT THE DIFFERENCE

Find the 7 differences in the pictures below.

Monkey Mind Manager

It's important to notice when you're feeling distracted and take a moment for yourself to help focus on the present moment. This might be when you're in a lesson, playing, or preparing for a test.

Fill in the juggling balls with all the thoughts in your head at the moment.

Which one of these things should you be focused on now? Colour in that juggling ball.

MINDFUL MAGIC

Given how busy our minds are, you might need to tame your monkey mind several times every day. That's OK, everyone does.

Distraction Danger Zones

Life is so full and busy that it is very easy to get distracted from what we should be doing. If you train your mind to spot when it is distracted, you can take action to refocus.

Make a list of things that might distract you. It could be things that you are worrying about (e.g. an argument or your homework), or things you are excited about (e.g. a party or a special treat).

1.

2.

3.

4.

5.

Now let's see what really distracts you. Keep a distraction diary for a week (or longer if you want). You might be surprised by the results!

MINDFUL MAGIC

Once you have identified your "distraction danger zones", make sure you check if you need to use one of the tools from your tool kit to stay focused.

Think about...

I was distracted by...

Where was I?

What was I doing?

What time was it?

Monday

_____
_____
_____
_____
_____
_____
_____
_____

Tuesday

_____
_____
_____
_____
_____
_____
_____
_____

Wednesday

_____
_____
_____
_____
_____
_____
_____
_____

Thursday

_____
_____
_____
_____
_____
_____
_____
_____

Friday

_____
_____
_____
_____
_____
_____
_____
_____

Saturday

_____
_____
_____
_____
_____
_____
_____
_____

Sunday

_____
_____
_____
_____
_____
_____
_____
_____

Now look back at all your entries and answer these questions.

I am most distracted in the: morning/ afternoon/ evening
(Circle the one that applies to you)

The things that distract me
most often are:

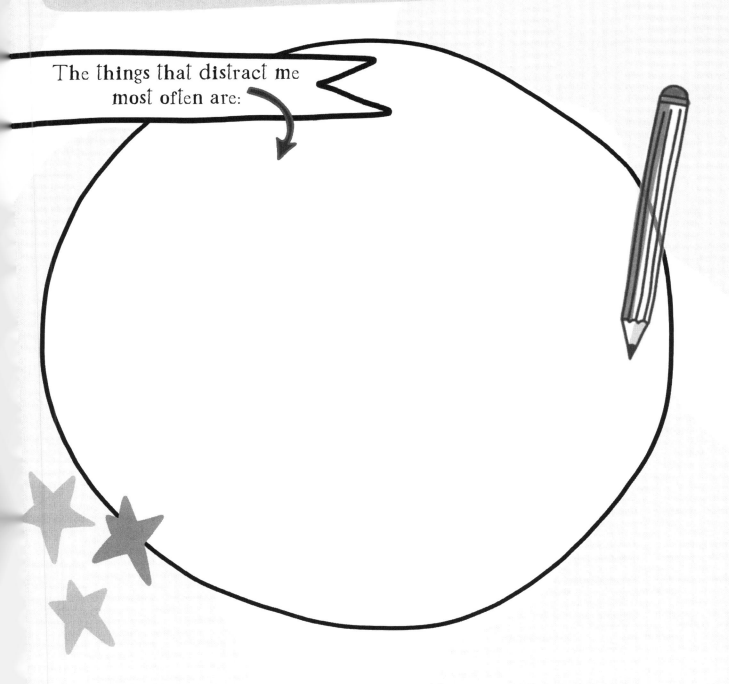

NOSY BREATHING

1. Find a quiet place where you can focus on yourself.

2. Sit comfortably on a chair, with your feet flat on the floor.

3. Close your eyes, or lower your gaze towards the ground.

4. Follow your breathing, let your tummy rise and fall.

5. With the other hand, use your finger to press one nostril closed and notice how your breath flows in and out through the open nostril.

6. Repeat for 5 breaths.

7. Let your nostril open again.

8. Switch hands and repeat with the other nostril.

9. Breathe in and out, notice the steady flow of breath through the open nostril.

10. Repeat for 5 breaths.

11. Let your nostril open again.

12. Place both hands on your lap and take 5 slow breaths through both nostrils.

13. Open your eyes, bringing your attention back to your surroundings.

Check in with yourself... How do you feel now?

MINDFUL MAGIC

When we practise balanced breathing, we allow our mind to focus on just that one thing, letting the noisy chatter of thoughts go away.

Congratulations!

You're going to need a bigger toolbox soon! These new tools help you to stop getting distracted and focus better.

In the Toolbox:

 Use your Monkey Mind Manager to de-clutter your thoughts.

Recognise your Distraction Danger Zones so you can take action.

Try Nosy Breathing to refocus.

You are now ready to use these tools anywhere!

Chapter 5

In this chapter we're going to:

- Consider how your body feels
- Improve your memory
- Use movement to refocus

Before we start, check in with yourself.

How does your body feel right now? Tingly, FUZZY, hot, calm, cold, shaky...

My body feels:

MINDFUL MAGIC · · · · · · · · · · · · ·
Your brain is a muscle and, just like every other muscle, exercise will make it bigger and stronger.

More Brain Science

The brain is fascinating: it controls everything we do, say, think, and much more!

We learned that there are four parts of the brain that are important in helping us be our best self!

We use special names for each part of the brain to help us remember its function:

 Pre frontal Cortex = Focus Function

 Hippocampus = Record Keeper

 Insula = Emotions Radar

 Amygdala = Survival Instinct

In this chapter, we're going to use the record keeper.

Your Spirit Animal

Close your eyes, sit comfortably with your hands resting on your knees. Think of an animal you love which has these traits:

Strong. Fast. Agile. Brave. Smart.

Imagine being part of that animal. Feel how it moves. Now breathe in and stretch your arms out above your head. Breathe out and let all the tension go from your arms, and body.

Open your eyes and draw your spirit animal.

MINDFUL MAGIC
Use the strength of your spirit animal to give you extra confidence.

KIM'S GAME

This game is named after Kim, a character in a book by Rudyard Kipling, who played it when he was training to be a spy!

You'll need your friends or family to play this game with.

How to play

1. Take turns to gather ten small objects from around the house, but don't let anyone else see them!

2. Hide them on the tray under the cloth.

3. When everyone is ready, lift the cloth and count to five. Then cover the tray up again.

4. Everyone else now has three minutes to write down or draw the items .

5. When time is up, remove the cloth and see what they scored.

6. You get one point for each correct item and a bonus point for any details they can remember – for example if there is a toy car, they get an extra point for remembering the colour of the car...

Equipment

- A tray
- A piece of cloth
- Pen and paper

Challenge: Next time, try adding more objects to the tray.

Which part of the brain helped you to remember the objects?

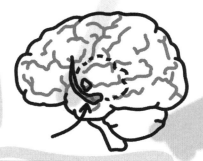

Listopedia

Lists help us remember things, tidying our brain, and making room for more learning.

You could cut these lists out and keep them in your pocket.

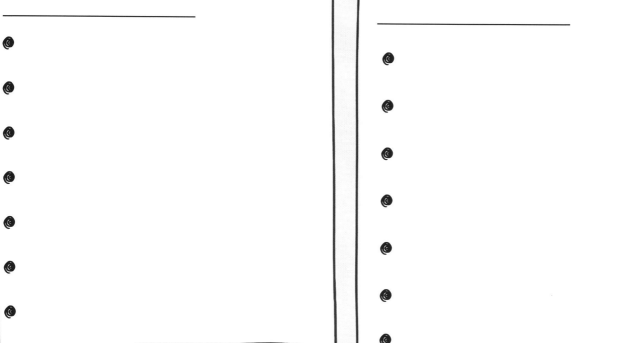

I NEED A LIST!

The Doodle-back Brain Workout

This activity needs a partner. It can be a friend or family member.

For this exercise, the person with shorter hair is going to be "A". The other person will be "B".

Person A sits in front, with their back to Person B, either on the floor or on stools.

Sit quietly and take a few deep breaths in through the nose and out through the mouth.

Chose a topic e.g. shapes / letters / animals / food / names.

Person B uses their index finger to write / draw on Person A's back. When the drawing is finished, Person B places their hand on Person A's shoulder.

Can Person A guess what was drawn on their back?

Now switch roles.

MINDFUL MAGIC
This is a fun way to train your brain, improve your focus, and boost your powers of concentration.

Shake, Rattle & Roll

Sometimes when we feel negative emotions, physically moving can shake them off.

1. Find a safe space to move.
2. Stand with your feet flat on the floor, shoulder width apart, arms by your side.
3. Begin to shake your hands.
4. Then shake your arms.
5. Keep going until your whole body is shaking like crazy.
6. Keeping your feet planted on the ground, bend your knees to start bouncing up and down.
7. Swing your arms forwards and backwards, like you're skiing.
8. Swing your arms round and round, like a helicopter.
9. After a few minutes, slow the motion, until you're standing completely still.
10. Take five deep breaths and smile.

Did you have to concentrate on the movements?

_____
_____
_____
_____
_____

How do you feel now?

_____
_____
_____
_____

Congratulations!

You have unlocked three more mindfulness tools! These help you to use your memory more effectively and focus on what's happening around you.

In the Toolbox:

 Play Kim's Game to improve your memory.

 Use Lists to reduce the pressure on your memory.

 Shake, Rattle and Roll your worries away.

You are now ready to use these tools anywhere!

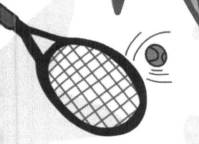

Chapter 6

In this chapter we're going to:

- Put all five senses to work
- Let nature calm you
- Improve your focus

Before we start, check in with yourself.

How are you feeling?

Choose a colour to represent how you feel.

Now colour in your thermometer.

ANGRY

TENSE

CALM

The first step to being self-aware is noticing how we are feeling in ourselves. Like paint splatters or snowflakes, everyone is different.

MINDFUL MAGIC

Feelings change throughout the day. Some feelings stay for a long time and some only for a short time.

Brain Science Quiz

Can you match the part of the brain to the correct function?

Insula	Emotions Radar
Amygdala	Focus Function
Pre Frontal Cortex	Record Keeper
Hippocampus	Survival Instinct

MINDFUL MAGIC

Did you know you're using your hippocampus to complete this challenge?

Flower Power

Take some time outside, looking at the plants around you.

You'll need either a flower press or a heavy book and some absorbent paper (e.g. blotting paper, a coffee filter paper).

Find a flower or leaf. (Note — if you're planning to pick flowers, always check you're allowed to beforehand.)

Put the flower or leaf in between two sheets of blotting paper and slip it inside the book.

Lay the book flat and leave it for three or four weeks. You can stack more books on top to add extra weight (or a tin of food works). It's ready when all the moisture has gone and it's papery.

You can put the dried flower/leaf in a photo frame or make it into a birthday card.

I HAVE THE POWER TO MAKE MY DREAMS COME TRUE

This page is perfect just as it is.

Aroma Armour

A sense of smell is unique to each individual. Some smells can have a positive effect on you, making you feel excited, happy, calm, etc. They can also send messages to your brain, reminding you of a positive memory you have. Other smells can have a negative effect on you. The scent can make you feel sick, angry, upset and can send a message to your brain reminding you of an unhappy memory.

Here are some typical reactions to scent:

	makes you feel	makes you think of
Flowers	Happy	Sunshine
Disinfectant	Sick	Hospitals

When you're not feeling happy or calm, try to surround yourself with scents that send messages to your brain to trigger positive memories.

The scents don't have to be physical, you can imagine them. Fill these bottles with your favourite smells.

Whenever you feel down, close your eyes and picture one of these bottles. Breathe deeply and recall the scent.

Fab Five Game

Find a safe place outside to play.

You can play this on your own or with friends.

Garden

Playground

Park

Beach

Lake

Forest

Sit or lie down, feel comfortable but not sleepy!
Close your eyes and concentrate on the sounds around you.
How many different sounds can you hear?
When you get to five sounds, shout "FAB FIVE!"
Open your eyes and make a note of all the sounds you heard.

Location: ....
1.
2.
3.
4.
5.

Location: ....
1.
2.
3.
4.
5.

Location: ....
1.
2.
3.
4.
5.

MINDFUL MAGIC

To make this more challenging and to use your Focus Function (Prefrontal Cortex), repeat the game but you have to find NEW sounds each time.

Five Senses Scavenger Hunt

One of the best ways to connect our mind and stay focused is by being aware of our surroundings. Use your senses to take in as much detail of your surroundings as possible.

Find five different smells.
1.
2.
3.
4.
5.

Which of these can you hear?

- [ ] A bird
- [ ] A plane
- [ ] A vehicle
- [ ] A voice
- [ ] A siren
- [ ] A telephone
- [ ] The wind
- [ ] Leaves rustling

Touch five different objects.

Something round? ....

Something smooth? ....

Something soft or fluffy? ....

Something cold? ....

Something fragile? ....

Draw four things you can see.

Think of your sense of taste. Which do you prefer?

- [ ] Chocolate
- [ ] Crisps

Be a Body Detective

Did you know your body will detect any emotion long before your mind?

It doesn't matter if it's a memory, something you're doing at the moment, or even if you're thinking about the future.

Recognising the clues your body feels will give you the power to be a body detective.

Mouth open

Wide eyes

Scared
Happy
Anxious
Worried
Confused
Nervous
Calm
Excited

Heart pounding

Fidgeting

Butterflies in your stomach

Feeling Sick

Bouncy feet

Sweaty hands

Wobbly Knees

Blushing

These clues can come from any part of the body. And they will be different for every person, so the clues your body gets might be different to your friends or family.

You might stamp your feet when you're angry, whilst someone else may clench their fists. Perhaps you curl into a ball when you're scared, whilst someone else may look at their feet.

Draw lines to join the body sensations to the hidden emotion.

There can be more than one line for each feeling.

Eyes widen

Head tilted down

Eyes facing down

Shoulders tighten

Sweaty palms

Weak knees / shaky legs

Clenched fists

Tingly legs

Feet hopping

Heart beating rapidly

Hot cheeks/ ears

Mouth wide open

Tears forming

Stomach rumbling

Anger

Sadness

Happy

Excited

Nervous

Worried

Calm

Scared

Upset

Lonely

Shocked

Anxious

Famished

Surprised

MINDFUL MAGIC

When you notice one of these sensations in your body, take a moment to recognise the emotion. Use the power of your mind to control your body.

The Scent of Silence

To coach your wandering mind into staying focused, you need to tune into all your senses.

Take a moment, wherever you are, to...

PAUSE

You could be sitting in your home, at school, in the playground, in the garden.

If you can, step out into nature and find a comfortable, safe place to sit for a moment.

1. Close your eyes.
2. Take a deep breath in and notice what sounds you can hear.
3. Breathe out, and on your next in breath notice what you can smell.
4. Continue to take three more deep breaths in and out.
5. Check in with how you feel now.

MINDFUL MAGIC

When your mind is distracted with too many thoughts, it's good to recognise this and bring your attention back. Try this exercise in different settings.

Congratulations!

Your toolbox is almost full now. These tools help you to use all your senses to be calmer, happier, and more focused.

In the Toolbox:

 Use your favourite Aroma Armour to change your mood.

 Be a Body Detective and recognise how physical reactions relate to your mood.

 Tune into different senses to focus your mind with the Scent of Silence.

You are now ready to use these tools anywhere!

Chapter 7

Become A
Happiness
Magnet

In this chapter we're going to:

- Use brain science

- Explore what happiness is

- Nurture your happy thoughts

Before we start, check in with yourself.

How are you feeling?

_____

Choose a colour to represent your emotion.

Now colour in the dot to match the emotion you want to feel.

MINDFUL MAGIC

If the colours don't match, use one of your existing tools and see if you can get them to match.

Expert Brain Science

You have learned about each part of the brain that can help you be your best self. Your best self is not like anyone else, you are unique!

Now you're an expert on your own brain, write down each time that you recognise when you have used one of these parts of the brain and think about how it helped you to do something.

Part of the brain	Symbol	Function	When did you use it? How did it help you?
Prefrontal cortex		Focus function	
Hippocampus		Record keeper	
Insula		Emotions radar	
Amygdala		Survival instinct	

Snowy Mountain

Unhappy thoughts and feelings can make you feel weak, angry, or worried. Did you know exercise helps refocus your mind? It doesn't need to be vigorous; any physical movement has the same effect.

- Find a peaceful and open space.

- Stand tall with your feet about shoulder-width apart.

- Stretch your hands up above your head.

- Picture yourself as a snow-capped mountain.

- Breathe in and reach your fingertips high.

- Breathe out and bring your hands all the way to the ground, wriggling your fingers like snowflakes falling softly on the mountain as you lower them.

- Breathe in and reach your hands up to the sky again.

- Repeat several times.

How do you feel after this exercise? Have you replaced your unwanted thoughts and feelings with fresh, white snow?

MINDFUL MAGIC

Visualising positive things can help you overcome unwanted feelings.

STRIKE A POSE

This game is best played with 2 or more people.
It's a great way to get moving and have some fun!

Take turns to be the call master.

The silliest pose (without making a sound or falling over) is the winner.
Everyone gets a vote!

Here are some ideas for things you could call out. Add your own to complete the list.

On your knees

Bunny hop

Stork legs

Jazz hands

Chicken wings

Funny faces

Puppy dog

Headstand

Crab walk

Choose Your Own Adventure

You have a choice which path you take, — THINK — before you — REACT.

Here are some scenarios that you might encounter.

Someone is unkind to you.

What would be a bad way to react?	What would be a better way to react?

You get a low score on one of your tests.

What would be a bad way to react?	What would be a better way to react?

You weren't picked for a team you wanted to be in.

What would be a bad way to react?	What would be a better way to react?

MINDFUL MAGIC

By using your Mindfulness Tools you have the power to choose your reaction.

Sunflower Strength

Everyday you'll have a range of feelings, which is normal. Try to savour the good moments and use them to grow your own happiness.

You Will Need:

- Several clean plant pots
- Decorating materials – paper, paint, fabric, ribbons, washi tape
- Glue
- Sticky tape
- Scissors
- Sunflower seeds
- Compost

Decorate the plant pots any way you like.

Plant one seed every day and think about the things that made you happy that day.

Now watch your sunflowers grow big and strong.

Don't forget to water them!

Feather Breathing

You'll need to find a feather before you can try this.

Stick your feather here when you're done:

1. Find somewhere out of the wind.
2. Lie on your back, legs straight, arms by your side.
3. Place a feather on your tummy.
4. Notice how the feather rises as you breathe in and falls as you breath out.
5. Breathe in and out ten times, focusing on the feather.

Congratulations!

You have unlocked the final three mindfulness tools for this book! These help you to be your happiest self.

In the Toolbox:

 Visualise a Snowy Mountain to fill your mind with fresh new thoughts.

 Choose your own adventure to follow.

Use Feather Breathing to connect your mind and body.

You are now ready to use these tools anywhere!

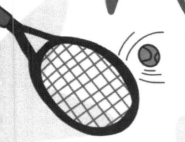

INDEX

All the activities in this book can be repeated, tick the ones you have tried.

Breathing

- [ ] Fingertip breathing
- [ ] Tense and release
- [ ] Snow angels
- [ ] Nosy breathing
- [ ] Shake, rattle, and roll
- [ ] Scent of silence
- [ ] Feather breathing

Visualisation

- [ ] Marvellous me potion
- [ ] Frame it
- [ ] Let it go
- [ ] Mischievous monkeys
- [ ] Your spirit animal
- [ ] Aroma armour
- [ ] Snowy mountain

Game

- [ ] Mindful wordsearch
- [ ] See into the future
- [ ] Mind maze
- [ ] Spot the difference
- [ ] Kim's game
- [ ] Fab five
- [ ] Strike a pose

Analysis

- [ ] All about me
- [ ] My zen zone
- [ ] Travelling thoughts
- [ ] Monkey mind manager
- [ ] Listopedia
- [ ] Five senses scavenger hunt
- [ ] Choose your own adventure

To do

- [ ] Goal tracker
- [ ] Lava lamp
- [ ] Transfiguration
- [ ] Mirror to your mind
- [ ] Distraction danger zones
- [ ] Doodle back
- [ ] Be a body detective
- [ ] Sunflower strength

Art

- [ ] Shine like the sun
- [ ] Doodle time
- [ ] Let it go
- [ ] Focus
- [ ] Wise owl
- [ ] Flower power
- [ ] Breathe
- [ ] Hope

Notes

BELIEVE IN YOURSELF

LEXI REES

Lexi was born in Edinburgh and grew up in the Scottish Highlands, although she now lives down south. When she's not writing or tutoring, she's a keen crafter and spends a considerable amount of time trying not to fall off horses or boats. She's usually covered in sand, straw, or glitter.

🏠 lexirees.co.uk   ⊙ lexi.rees

SASHA MULLEN

Sasha has always had a passion for adventure. Be it experiencing the sights, sounds and smells of far flung continents to exploring her hometown of West London. Letting her senses guide her head or heart, she has utilised her personal experiences to gather a kaleidoscope of skills. How to embrace a teaching role in New York- a city so vast and vibrant, how to cope with grief and transition into motherhood. Being a teacher in primary schools since 2010 has enabled her to see the need for incorporating Mindfulness practice into everyday education. When Sasha is not teaching or enjoying her family or socialising with friends, she is taking an exercise class, and is particularly fond of the child's pose in yoga, when she can happily have a power snooze!

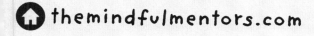 themindfulmentors.com   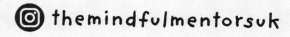 themindfulmentorsuk

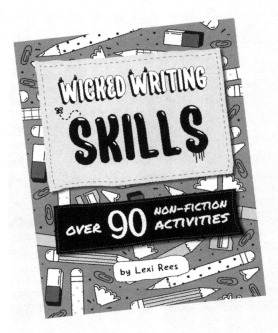

MT. ACONCAGUA
ARGENTINA / HEIGHT: 22,840 FEET / 6,962 METERS

MT. DENALI
(MCKINLEY) - UNITED STATES (ALASKA)
HEIGHT: 20,310 FEET / 6,190 METERS

MT. ELBRUS
RUSSIA / HEIGHT: 18,510 FEET / 5,642 METERS

MT. EVEREST
NEPAL/TIBET
HEIGHT: 29,032 FEET / 8,849 METERS

THE SEVEN SUMMITS

These mountains represent the highest peaks on each of the seven continents. Climbing all seven is a major goal for mountaineers worldwide.

MT. KILIMANJARO
TANZANIA / HEIGHT: 19,341 FEET / 5,895 METERS

MT. KOSCIUSZKO
AUSTRALIA (MAINLAND)
HEIGHT: 7,310 FEET / 2,228 METERS

MT. VINSON
ANTARCTICA / HEIGHT: 16,050 FEET / 4,892 METERS

MOUNT ELBRUS

KREMENA SPENGLER

CREATIVE EDUCATION • CREATIVE PAPERBACKS

Published by Creative Education and Creative Paperbacks
P.O. Box 227, Mankato, Minnesota 56002
Creative Education and Creative Paperbacks
are imprints of The Creative Company
www.thecreativecompany.us

Design by Graham Morgan
Art direction by Blue Design (www.bluedes.com)

Images by Dreamstime/Aleksandr Rybalko, 38–39, E. Malakhovskaya, 6,
Extezy, 1, Katalinks, 43, Konstantin Shishkin, 24, Konstantin Mezhuritskiy, 32,
Ktree, 22, Panaramka, 37, Pavel Sytilin, 33, Pecorb, cover, 1, Vladislav Astanin,
36, Wrangel, 20, Zefart, 2; Flickr/Biodiversity Heritage Library, 14; Getty
Images/Anton Petrus, 14–15, Anton Petrus, 18, Gleb Tarro, 21, Milo Zanecchia/
Ascent Xmedia, 4–5, 9, Nastasic, 10, Supachai Panyaviwat, 13, ullstein bild Dtl.,
35; Wikimedia Commons/Anna Shalashova, 40, Compte fermé, 28, Dmitry A.
Mottl, 31, Giles Laurent, 16, Loïc Perrin, 26, NKBV, 45, NPS/Neal Herbert, 17,
Salerson at English Wikipedia, 44, Sebnem Gulfidan, 25, Гвоздев Ростислав
Станиславович, 29

Library of Congress Cataloging-in-Publication Data
Names: Spengler, Kremena, author.
Title: Mount Elbrus / Kremena Spengler.
Description: Mankato, Minnesota : Creative Education and Creative
   Paperbacks, [2025] | Series: The seven summits | Includes
   bibliographical references and index. | Audience: Ages 10–14 | Audience:
   Grades 4–6 | Summary: "Mount Elbrus, an extinct volcano, is Europe's
   tallest peak and a Seven Summits mountaineering challenge. This guide
   for kids age 12 and up examines the mountain's geologic and climbing
   history. Includes a glossary, sidebars, profiles of notable climbers,
   and further resources"—Provided by publisher.
Identifiers: LCCN 2024030264 (print) | LCCN 2024030265 (ebook) | ISBN
   9798889892717 (library binding) | ISBN 9781682776377 (paperback) | ISBN
   9798889893820 (ebook)
Subjects: LCSH: Elbrus, Mount (Russia)—Juvenile literature. |
   Mountaineering—Russia (Federation)—Elbrus, Mount, Region—Juvenile
   literature.
Classification: LCC GB542.R9 S64 2025 (print) | LCC GB542.R9 (ebook) |
   DDC 796.52209475/2—dc23/eng/20240712
LC record available at https://lccn.loc.gov/2024030264
LC ebook record available at https://lccn.loc.gov/2024030265

Printed in the United States of America

Mount Elbrus remains snow-capped in summer, even as the land around it turns green.

CONTENTS

INTRODUCTION

The mountain "hotel" looked like a gigantic Airstream travel trailer. Perched on a ridge between two glaciers at 13,780 feet (4,200 meters), Priyut 11 could sleep up to 200 people—all of them climbers headed to Europe's tallest peak: Mount Elbrus.

Early one morning in August 1989, a group left this metal-clad refuge under a thick canopy of stars. Upwind, a lightning storm illuminated distant peaks. Just before sunrise, as the climbers passed 16,000 feet (4,877 m), the winds picked up. By the time they reached the Elbrus saddle at 17,769 feet (5,416 m), a furious hailstorm hit. Visibility dropped to 15 feet (4.6 m). Fortunately, the guide knew the mountain well. He found a hole in the ice from which warm gasses escaped, called a fumarole. The climbers huddled inside it. After an hour, they decided to retreat.

The group tried for Mount Elbrus's summit again the next day. And despite the cold, stiff wind, they reached the top! Below, peaks of the Caucasus Mountains poked through the clouds, stretching for hundreds of miles. The Black Sea sparkled for a moment in the west, then vanished in the mist. For 10 minutes, the group sat in exhausted, awed silence. As they headed back, the snow achieved "a perfect slipperiness." Launching themselves down the slopes in sitting positions, the climbers used their ice axes as rudders and hollered with joy.

For safety reasons, climbing Mount Elbrus as part of a team is best.

An antique map of the Caucasus highlights the region's mountainous terrain in brown.

CHAPTER 1: EUROPE'S TALLEST PEAK

ount Elbrus is in the Caucasus Mountains, a long, steep spine connecting the Black and Caspian seas. The range is split among Russia, Georgia, Armenia, and Azerbaijan. Along with the Urals to the north, it is historically considered the boundary between Europe and Asia. The region within which the range lies is called the Caucasus.

Mount Elbrus is in the Russian republic of Kabardino-Balkaria, just north of the Georgian border. The Black Sea is 60 miles (97 kilometers) to its west and the Caspian Sea about 230 miles (370 km) to its east. On clear days, the Black Sea is visible from the summit. Elbrus is at the center of Prielbrusye National Park, which was formed in 1986. The mountain is the highest point in Russia and all of Europe. It is one of the Seven Summits and is the world's 10th most prominent peak. Prominence is not the same as height; it measures the distance one needs to descend from the top before starting to climb again.

Mount Elbrus is an inactive, or dormant, volcano that is approximately 2.5 million years old. The volcano's last known eruption was in 50 C.E. It actually has two peaks (also called summits, cones, or domes). The west dome rises to 18,510 feet (5,642 m), and the east to 18,356 feet (5,595 m). Between them is a saddle that dips to 17,769 feet (5,416 m). The peaks are snow-and-ice-filled craters. Although Elbrus is dormant, high volcanic activity is being recorded inside it. Hot lava heats water up to 140 degrees Fahrenheit (60 degrees Celsius), feeding the mineral springs of the popular neighboring spa towns of Pyatigorsk, Kislovodsk, and Mineralnye Vody (Mineral Waters).

Much of Mount Elbrus is covered by ice. More than 20 main glaciers and 77 secondary glaciers are found on the mountain. Water from glacier melts feeds surrounding rivers. The Baksan, Kuban, and Malka flow from the Elbrus glaciers, irrigating the farmland and plains to the north. Glacial action has created several tiny but deep lakes. But the glaciers are in retreat. Over the past century, their size has decreased by 18 percent.

Mount Elbrus is cold. Even in summer, night temperatures are around 18°F (-8°C). In the snow-capped areas, temperatures fall to as low as -22°F (-30°C). In winter, they drop to -58°F (-50°C) at the summit. Weather is harsher on the western side of the mountain. Because Elbrus is in the Northern Hemisphere, summer runs from June to mid-September. Half the days are sunny, on average. But strong winds can turn violent suddenly and lead to a temperature drop. Winds of more than 60 miles (97 km) per hour are not unusual. At elevations above 13,000 feet (3,962 m), blizzards strike even in summer. The amount of precipitation rises with height. The lower elevations receive about 20 inches

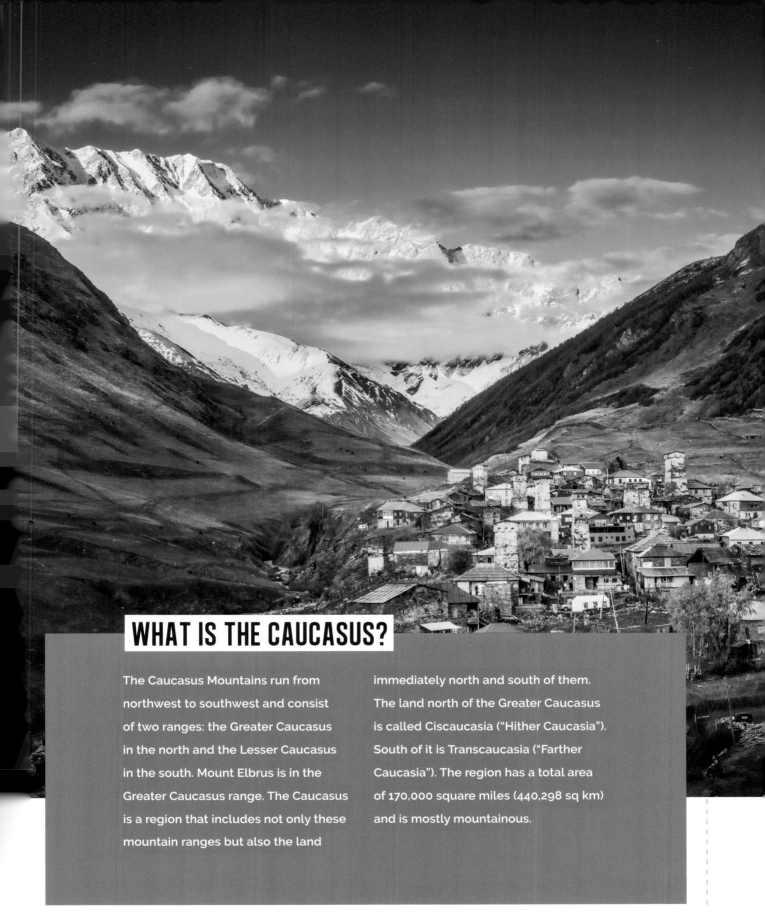

WHAT IS THE CAUCASUS?

The Caucasus Mountains run from northwest to southwest and consist of two ranges: the Greater Caucasus in the north and the Lesser Caucasus in the south. Mount Elbrus is in the Greater Caucasus range. The Caucasus is a region that includes not only these mountain ranges but also the land immediately north and south of them. The land north of the Greater Caucasus is called Ciscaucasia ("Hither Caucasia"). South of it is Transcaucasia ("Farther Caucasia"). The region has a total area of 170,000 square miles (440,298 sq km) and is mostly mountainous.

THE SEVEN SUMMITS

MOUNT ELBRUS

(51 centimeters) annually, while the higher elevations receive 60 inches (152 cm).

The Caucasus is the meeting point of Central/Northern Europe, Central Asia, and the Middle East/North Africa. As a result, the region supports a wide variety of life. Like other alpine ecosystems, Mount Elbrus has a mixture of evergreen forests, grasslands, and alpine meadows. They are home to many birds, mammals, and other animals. The area has 12,000 species of plants, of which more than 1,000 are found only there. It has 700 species of vertebrate (backboned) animals, of which 70 live only there.

With its ever-present cap of snow, Elbrus cools the national park around it, supporting plants which usually grow in cooler climate zones. At the highest elevation at which plants can still grow, lichens cling to the rock faces. Whitlow grasses and flowering plants called saxifrages peek out among the lichens. In the alpine belt just below, grasses grow to 6 inches

(15 cm) tall. Further down, in the subalpine meadows, grasses and flowers grow as tall as 30 inches (76 cm). One of the region's loveliest flowering shrubs, the Caucasian rhododendron, grows in this zone. The locals call it "the alpine rose." Its pale pink and cream-colored blossoms bloom in early spring. The plant digs its roots deep into the thin soil of the steep slopes, which allows it to survive beneath 5 feet (1.5 m) of snow.

Young chamois are born in late spring, when grasses and other plants are plentiful.

Foxes hear prey moving beneath the snow and then pounce to break the icy crust.

Birches grow in the park's forests. So do Caucasian and Scots pines. One rare species of birch is a relic from 65 million years ago. It has pink bark and dark green leaves. The high mountain forests are rich in mushrooms and wild berries, too.

Chamois, a kind of wild mountain goat-antelope, live at the borders of alpine meadows and forests, feeding on grasses and young trees. Higher in the mountains live turs, another goat-antelope species with huge curved horns. Turs rest in groups of 8 to 10 during the day, coming out to graze in the alpine meadows in the evening. In winter, turs form larger herds and head toward the valleys. It is a difficult time of year for them. Food is hard to find, and many fall prey to wolves.

Foxes also hunt in the park around Mount Elbrus, catching small rodents such as wood mice and voles. Lynxes prey on Caucasian snowcocks and other birds, hares, roe deer, turs, and chamois. Caucasian red deer, one of the largest deer species, roam the park. Brown bears live throughout the forests but are especially common in the Baksan River valley. They can sometimes be seen in the early morning, drinking from the mineral springs. Weasels and wild boars are common, too. The Caucasian leopard is now critically endangered, with just 1,300 left in the wild. Wildlife in the region, especially in the native forests, is threatened by logging, urban growth, and poor wilderness management.

From Elbrus's slope, the Caucasus Mountains look beautiful and foreboding at the same time.

CHAPTER 2: MYTHICAL MOUNTAIN

Elbrus is a mountain with many names, and it features in the stories of many groups of people. The oldest name comes from ancient Persian (Iranian) legends. They mention a mountain called Hara Berezaiti, around which the stars and planets revolved. The name means "high sentinel, guard, or watchpost." As the Persian language changed, Hara Berezaiti became Harborz, which became Alborz (or Elburz). Elbrus is a version of Alborz; it is also the name of a long mountain range in northern Iran. The Greek historian Arrian named the peak Strobilos, which is Latin for "twisted object," such as a pine cone. This name likely reflects Elbrus's shape.

The Balkars and Karachays are Turkic people who live near Mount Elbrus. They call it Mingi-Tau. In Balkarian, it means "a thousand mountains." Local Turkic people also call the area Yalbuz, or "ice mane." In their legends, magical creatures gathered on these "bald mountains." A nearby Northwest Caucasian

MOUNT ELBRUS

ZEUS

group, the Circassians (Cherkess), called the peak Oshkhamakhua—"mountain of happiness."

Whatever its name, Mount Elbrus is perhaps best known through an ancient Greek myth. Prometheus, a titan and a clever trickster, stole fire from the god Zeus and gave it to humans. Zeus became very angry, so he chained Prometheus to Elbrus as punishment and sent an eagle to peck on his liver. Even worse, the liver re-grew every night, and the eagle returned each day to torment Prometheus. Fortunately, but only after many years, the hero Heracles (Hercules) freed Prometheus and killed the eagle with an arrow.

Mount Elbrus also has ties to the Bible. Some local stories claim Noah's ark first ran aground on Mount Elbrus, before settling on Mount Ararat several hundred miles to the south (in today's Turkey). As it broke free from Elbrus, the bottom of the ark split the mountain in two, creating its twin peaks.

These legends highlight the region's human diversity. The Caucasus was a major land route north for ancient civilizations in the Middle East. The mountain peoples of the Caucasus were overrun by the Huns, the Mongols, the Turks, and the Russians. Smaller groups, under pressure from stronger neighbors, sought refuge in the ravines of the mountain ranges. As a result, a greater variety of languages is spoken in the Caucasus than in any other area of similar size in the world.

More than 50 ethnic groups inhabit the Caucasus. Russians and Ukrainians speak Slavic languages of the Indo-European family. The language of the Armenians is Indo-European but different from other languages in this family.

PUNISHMENT FROM THE GODS

According to an old Balkar folktale, the Balkar people came down to Earth from a constellation called the She-Bear. They were meant to live in peace with the mountain Mingi-Tau and the gods who ruled from it. The gods welcomed the Balkars but forbid them from climbing the tall peaks. They punished those who dared disobey this rule with headaches and hallucinations. These problems are now known to be symptoms of **altitude sickness** and breathing in sulphuric gasses that escape from cracks in the mountain's surface.

KABARDA HORSES

Kabardas are sturdy, medium-sized horses that are usually black, bay, or gray. Families in the Greater Caucasus have bred them since at least the 1500s. The horses carried warriors battling Russian forces in the 1800s, and their strength and endurance were legendary. But when the Soviet Union collapsed in 1991, local horse farms were left with thousands of horses but no money to feed them or pay worker salaries. A few breeders and trainers managed to set up stables outside Russia. Their horses have competed in grueling races, some as long as 100 miles (161 km), in Europe and the Middle East.

Other groups speak Indo-European languages of the Iranian branch. Most people, however, speak languages of the Caucasian family, although there seems to be no connection between South Caucasian and North Caucasian languages. These languages are also distinct from the Turkic group.

Kabardino-Balkaria, where Mount Elbrus is located, lies in the center of the Greater Caucasus, occupying its highest part and nearby plains. The republic has an area of about 4,800 square miles (12,432 sq km), of which 70 percent is mountains. Its population includes Kabardins, Balkars, and Russians. The Kabardin are a Caucasian ethnicity closely related to the neighboring Circassian (Cherkess) group. Their language is North Caucasian. The written language uses the Cyrilic (Russian) alphabet. The Balkars are a Turkic people related to the neighboring Karachay. Their written language is also written in Cyrillic. Both Kabardins and Balkars are mostly Muslims. The Kabardins, who mostly live in the Kabardin Plain, became allies of the Russians as early as the 1550s. The Balkars of the high mountains, however, long fought the Russian conquerors.

In the 1800s, Russia conquered the Caucasus. Russian soldiers killed many villagers and stole their property. When a group called the Bolsheviks took power in Russia in 1917, they made the Balkar people abandon their traditional way of life and forced them to join collective farms.

During World War II (1939-45), Soviet and German troops fought for control of the region. The Germans wanted to conquer the rich oil fields south

A monument honors those who defended the Caucasus region during World War II.

Sunflowers are grown mostly for their seed oil, which is used in the food industry.

of the Caucasus. They occupied Mount Elbrus and the area around it for about six months. The Soviet Army pushed the Germans back in 1943, but Soviet leader Joseph Stalin accused the Balkars of helping Germany. The young Balkar men were actually at the front, fighting against the Germans, but Stalin sent the remaining Balkar villagers away, to Central Asia. Only about half of them returned to their homes after the war. The rest stayed in Central Asia or died on the way back.

The economy of Kabardino-Balkaria is based on farming, mining, manufacturing, and tourism. People in the Kabardin plain grow traditional crops such as wheat and sunflowers. Peaches, apples, and pears grow in the orchards. The mountain people herd goats and sheep. Horse breeders in the region today are trying to bring back the hardy horses for which their homeland was known in the past. Metal deposits in the Malka River Valley support mining. Factories in the cities make oil drilling equipment for nearby oil fields. They also make construction materials, such as glass and cement, and everyday consumer goods, such as shoes and clothing. The mountain rivers power hydroelectric power plants. Visitors come to climb and ski.

Despite this economic activity and the region's beauty, Kabardino-Balkaria is relatively poor and unstable. Many people are unemployed and rely on government assistance. Crime rates are high, and the region has a history of kidnappings. The Kabardins and Balkars do not always get along. War in nearby Chechnya in the early 2000s has made visitors reluctant to travel to the region.

Not all deep cracks in the mountainside are as easy to see as this one.

CHAPTER 3: CLIMBING ELBRUS

hile technically not a very difficult climb, Mount Elbrus is also not one to underestimate. An average of 15 to 30 climbers a year die on the mountain—a high ratio of climbers to climber deaths compared to other mountains. In 2004, the death toll reached 48! The elevation and the unpredictable weather make the climb a challenge. At the peak, the air contains only about half the oxygen available at sea level. Normal activities such as walking can take an extreme effort.

Many deaths are caused by a sudden change in weather. A climber may become confused by a snow squall and fall into one of the hidden crevasses off the route. Icefalls, too, can hurt climbers. It is advised to climb the peak in summer, from mid-May to mid-September, but especially July or August. While this is the busiest time, the temperatures are most bearable. Sudden storms are also less likely.

Mount Elbrus is a challenge that should be taken seriously. Mountaineers must prepare for all possible obstacles. They should bring a helmet, harness, ropes, ice axes, crampons, trekking poles, boots, sleeping bags, warm clothes, and sun protection. Campers will need tents, cooking equipment, utensils, and waste collection items.

Following the busiest routes is the safest way to avoid dangers, but preparation is also important. To prevent altitude sickness, at least a week should be spent at somewhat lower elevations before attempting to climb the peak. Cheget Peak, at 11,814 feet (3,601 m), is often used for this purpose. It also offers views of the Standard/South Route that many climbers choose to follow.

While there are at least 10 routes, the Standard Route is the most popular and busiest route to the top. On some days, as many as 100 climbers take it. As a result, reservations should be made well in advance. This route is well marked by bamboo wands.

The Standard Route uses a unique system of cable cars that runs from the Azaou road, at 7,152 feet (2,180 m), to just short of the Barrel Huts, at 12,795 feet (3,900 m). From the Barrel Huts, the route climbs to the Diesel Hut (formerly Priyut 11), then on to Pastukhov Rocks. The route then climbs to the saddle between the domes and on to the western summit. The elevation change on the ascent is 5,719 feet (1,743 m). There is also a track vehicle called a snowcat to take climbers up to 15,750 feet (4,800 m). Usually, climbers begin the challenge around 2 a.m. to be sure of reaching the summit by 11 a.m. and

MINERALNYE VODY

GETTING THERE

The airports nearest Mount Elbrus are Mineralnye Vody, which is 120 miles (193 km) away, and Nalchik, at 75 miles (121 km). Flights arrive from Moscow, St. Petersburg, and a few other Russian cities. Trains run from major Russian cities to Mineralnye Vody, Pyatigorsk, and Nalchik.

It is a three- to four-hour drive from Mineralnye Vody to Terskol, the village in the Baksan Valley nearest Elbrus. There are no regular public buses, so it is necessary to rent private transportation. A local bus does run from Nalchik, but its schedule can be unreliable.

returning before nightfall. The recommended times are six to nine hours up and three to six hours down.

Unfortunately, the Standard Route is known for being dirty. Climbers in the past have failed to follow the carry in/carry out rule. Most of the huts are primitive, and the toilets are terrible. Before burning down in 1998, the Priyut 11 had what *Outside* magazine ranked the "nastiest outhouse in the world."

The East Route to the peak is longer and quieter. It begins in the town of Elbrus and follows the Irikchat Gorge to the Irikchat Pass and the edge of the Elbrus glacial shield. Then it heads up the Irikchat Valley, climbing surrounding smaller peaks. The longer route helps climbers acclimatize over the course of a week. The route then heads straight up the lava flow across steep, snowy slopes and bands of rock near the top. It ends up on the eastern summit. The descent can be a retracing of steps or heading down the Standard Route.

A third way, the North Route, is more difficult, requiring sections of climbing with ropes. It begins on the Ullukol glacier, with Base Camp at 8,202 feet (2,500 m) and High Camp at 12,467 feet (3,800 m). It is a popular route for adventurers wanting to ski back down. It's also the least busy of the main Mount Elbrus routes. There are no huts on either the East or the North routes.

Most people arrive in the local area by plane or overnight train from Moscow to Mineralnye Vody. It is also possible to fly in from Dubai, United Arab Emirates, and Istanbul, Turkey, on some days. From Mineralnye Vody, it is

The Standard Route up Mount Elbrus, with elevations in meters

West summit, 5642

East summit, 5621

Slanting shelf, 5320

Pastukhov rocks, 4630

Shelter of eleven, 4050

Rescue station

"Garabashi" station & upper barrels, 3850

Lower barrels, 3700

UP, UP, UP

Three ski lifts transport Mount Elbrus guests. The first was built in 1959 and renovated in 2006. It begins at the Azaou road, at 7,152 feet (2,180 m) above sea level, and goes on to the Old Viewpoint, at 9,744 feet (2,970 m). The second, completed in 1976 and rebuilt in 2009, leads to the Mir station, at 11,385 feet (3,470 m). The last leg, finished in 2015, is a single-seat chairlift which saves hikers an hour-long trek from Mir to the Barrel Huts. Ending at an elevation of 12,621 feet (3,847 m), it's the second highest chairlift in Europe (after one in Switzerland).

about four hours by road to the south-side base camp and slightly longer to the north-side base camp.

Travel to Mount Elbrus became more dangerous after 1991. The breakdown of the Soviet Union led to instability. Russia fought two very bloody wars to suppress an independence drive in Chechnya. The U.S. government advised Americans against traveling to the Greater Caucasus, due to the risk of terrorism and other threats.

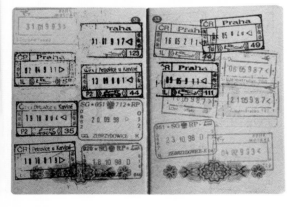

In February 2022, Russia invaded neighboring Ukraine, and it has waged a brutal war on that country since. The United States supports Ukraine, and as a result, Americans are very strongly warned not to travel to any part of Russia. U.S. citizens are likely to be harassed or wrongly arrested. Local law is enforced randomly. Flights into and out of Russia are very limited.

Even at the best of times, visiting Russia requires a passport, a visa (authorization to enter Russia), border zone and national park permits, police registration, and other formalities. Russia is known for red tape, slow and difficult visa processing, language barriers, and limited domestic travel options. If they go, Westerners are advised to hire a Russian adventure company, which can help them get the right documents and permissions.

MOUNT ELBRUS

CHAPTER 4: CONQUERORS OF ELBRUS

n July 22, 1829, Killar Khashirov, a Kabardin guide for a Russian army scientific expedition, became the first person to reach the lower, eastern peak of Mount Elbrus. Dangerous weather kept everyone but Khashirov from reaching the summit that day. But the expedition celebrated his feat with three-gun salutes and awarded him a prize of 400 silver rubles.

In 1874, the higher, western summit was scaled by Akhia Sottaiev, a Balkar guide for a group of British and Swiss explorers. Led by British climber Florence Crauford Grove, this expedition included Englishmen Frederick Gardner and Horace Walker, and Swiss climber Peter Knubel.

Andrey Pastukhov, a Russian military mapmaker, was first to climb both Elbrus summits. He reached the western dome unguided in 1890 and the eastern peak in 1896. Pastukhov also mapped this area in detail.

German soldiers took control of Mount Elbrus for a brief time during World War II.

MOUNTAIN HUTS

The most notable huts on Mount Elbrus are the aptly named Barrel Huts (also called the Barrels or Garabashi Station). Located at 12,795 feet (3,900 m) and considered the starting point for a summit attempt, the huts were originally barrel-shaped oil tanks. They have little more than mattresses, pillows, and crude toilets. Some have heaters, but the intense cold can affect their functioning. LEAPrus 3912, a hotel complex made by an Italian company, is an upgrade. The tube-shaped buildings are advertised as a top glamping (glamorous camping) accommodation, complete with Wi-Fi, indoor plumbing, and a dining hall.

Weather can change without warning on Elbrus, leading to heavy snowfall and poor visibility.

Mountaineering became a popular public pastime during the early years of the Soviet Union, and there was a lot of traffic on Mount Elbrus. In 1929, 11 Soviet scientists built the first small hut at 13,650 feet (4,161 m) and called it Priyut 11. A larger hut for 40 people was built there in 1932. A wilderness lodge was constructed in the saddle between the two summits in 1933, but it burned down after only a few years. Its ruins are still visible. On March 17, 1936, a party of 33 novice Komsomol (communist youth) members tried the peak and were killed when they slid on the ice and fell to their deaths.

In 1939, the Soviet tourist organization built another structure on Mount Elbrus. Coated in aluminum siding, it sat slightly above the first Priyut 11 location, at 13,780 feet (4,200 m). It was meant to accommodate Western visitors on guided trips who paid in foreign money. But not long after, this refuge was turned into a World War II mountain barracks, acting as a base for both Soviet and German forces during the Battle of the Caucasus.

In 1942, German forces occupied the land north of the Baksan Valley, taking the mountain valleys in the western Caucasus. The German army's 1st (Edelweiss, Alpine) Division occupied Priyut 11. After about six months, the Germans retreated, and by mid-February 1943, Elbrus was back under Soviet

THE SEVEN SUMMITS

MOUNT ELBRUS

control. One Soviet pilot even won a medal of honor for bombing the German fuel supply but leaving Priyut 11 intact.

The Soviet Union continued to sponsor Mount Elbrus ascents, and in 1956, a group of 400 mountaineers climbed to the top to mark the 400th anniversary of Kabardino-Balkaria. A cable car system carrying guests as high as 11,385 feet (3,470 m) was completed between 1959 and 1976.

n 1998, a group of climbers started a fire while cooking and accidentally burned down Priyut 11. In the summer of 2001, its replacement, the Diesel Hut, was erected. It was so named because it is on the site of a former diesel-powered generating station.

Thousands of people climb Mount Elbrus each year. New climbers come up with all kinds of challenges to make their attempt stand out: snowboarding down the mountain, motorcycling, and even driving a car up the slopes.

A Karachay horse team summits Mount Elbrus on September 4, 2020.

In 1997, Russian adventurer Alexander Abramov drove a Land Rover to the summit with a 10-member team. This adventure made Elbrus the highest mountain climbed by a vehicle and earned it a Guinness World Record title. The "drive" took about 40 days. The team had to change tires and go up and down the mountain to find lost parts because the car kept falling apart. The team was able to drive it up to the Barrel Huts but had to use a pulley system the rest of the way, reaching the top on September 13. Unfortunately, a driver lost control of the vehicle on the way down and had to jump out. He survived, but the car fell into the rocks. The team later returned to pull it out but found it impossible. The car remains below the peak.

n August 1998, climbers from the Karachay-Cherkess Republic became the first to ride horses up the mountain. The Karachay horses, named Imbir, Daur, and Khurzuk, wore special horseshoes with steel spikes. Six people reached the eastern summit: Karachay horsemen Dahir Kappushev, Mohammed Bidzhiev, and Murat Dzhatdoev, and Ingush mountaineers Boris Begeulov, Umar Bairamukov, and Leila Albogachieva. The same riders climbed the higher western summit in August 1999 with horse Igilik.

Horses and riders would try Mount Elbrus again 20 years later. In 2019, the Karachay horseman Aslan Khubiev and Balkar guides Aslan Altuev and Askhat Guzoev climbed with horses Boz and Damly. On September 4, 2020, Karachay riders Ramazan Alchakov and Abrek Ediev and Russian Ivan Kulaga reached

the western dome with horses Almaz and Dzhigit. On September 23, 2020, Karachay riders Taulan Achabaev and Rustam Achabaev and Balkar guide Aslan Altuev did the same with stallion Bahr.

Since then, other adventurers have completed their own unique climbs. In 2016, Russians Artyom Kuimov and Sergey Baranov set another Guinness world record by riding ATVs to the top of Mount Elbrus. In 2020, British climber Akke Rahman completed a charity climb for the Global Relief Trust. He managed it in one day, without preparation or oxygen, just days after recovering from a COVID-19 infection. Aida Tabelinova, a Kazakh scientist, climbed Mount Elbrus in October 2021 to promote international cooperation.

The peak of Mount Elbrus calls to young and old alike. An eight-year old Indian boy named Gandham Bhuvan Jai reached the top in September 2021, while Balkar guides tell stories of ancestors who climbed it hundreds of times and lived well past 100 years old. Like other tall peaks around the world, Elbrus awakens a spirit of challenge and adventure that will endure forever.

Like the Priyut 11 toilet, this private research station outhouse on Elbrus makes "going" an adventure.

BACK TO BASICS

Harold Tomb, a writer for *The New York Times*, climbed Mount Elbrus in 1989. He described Priyut 11, the mountain's metal-clad "hotel." "When the sun is up," he wrote, "water flows from a pipe stuck directly into the glacier above the hotel. Ice can be melted on the stove when the water isn't flowing." Referring to the hut's infamous toilet, he said, "The low temperatures make plumbing impossible, and trying to dig a hole in the volcanic rock or glacier ice would be pointless. The outhouse, therefore, must hang over the edge of a cliff, and every visit there is an adventure."

STORIES OF THE SUMMIT

KAISYN KULIEV

Kaisyn Shuvayevich Kuliev (1917–85) was a famous Balkarian poet. His poems were written in the Karachay-Balkarian language but translated into 140 others. Kaisyn was born in Nalchik, Russia, in the foothills of the Caucasus Mountains. He wrote his first poem when he was only 10 years old. He learned Russian and attended college in Moscow, then came back to his homeland to teach literature.

In 1940, Kaisyn was drafted by the Soviet Army and sent to fight in World War II. He served as a paratrooper and a war reporter and was wounded in battle more than once. During this time, he wrote several patriotic poems that were published in major Soviet newspapers.

In the early 1940s, Soviet leader Joseph Stalin accused the Balkars of helping the Germans and forced them out of the country. Kaisyn's influential friends in Moscow arranged for him to be allowed to live in Moscow when he returned from the war, but he decided, instead, to follow his people and live in Kyrgyzstan. Kaisyn was banned from publishing his own poems while there, so he translated other people's poetry instead.

After Stalin's death, many Balkars, including Kaisyn, returned to their homes. Kaisyn published several poetry collections, which blended Balkar, Russian, and Western poetic traditions. He received several awards for his contributions to Soviet poetry. When he died, he was buried in the garden of his house, which is now a museum. A street in Nalchik bears his name.

ELBRUS SKYRUNNERS

Skyrunning is running very high in the mountains. Its focus is on elevation gain and technicality. There are reportedly 200 official skyrunning races worldwide, with around 50,000 participants from 65 countries.

The Red Fox Elbrus Race was first held on Mount Elbrus in 2008. It is a festival that takes place from May 1 to May 9. According to organizers, the festival attracts about 500 participants and more than 1,000 spectators each year.

The festival has several parts. The Vertical Kilometer is a qualifying event in which runners attain an elevation of 1 kilometer (0.6 mile) as they cover a distance of no more than 5 kilometers (3 miles.) The men's Vertical Kilometer record was set by Vitaly Chernov, of Russia, in 2017. He ran it in 43 minutes, 14.6 seconds. The women's record—48 minutes, 31 seconds—was set by Russia's Elena Kravchenko in 2021.

During the "classic" race, skyrunners race from the Barrels to the top of the summit. The "classic" men's record belongs to Russia's Mikhail Klimov. At 2 hours, 27 minutes, 5 seconds, it remains unbeaten since 2010. Oksana Stefanishina of Russia holds the women's record of 2 hours, 48 minutes, 40 seconds, set in 2017.

The festival also features a professional "sport" category, in which runners reach the summit from Azaou Glade. The record holders are Karl Eglof, of Ecuador, with 3 hours, 24 minutes, 14 seconds (2017) and Anna Ogloblina, of Kyrgyzstan, with 4 hours, 17 minutes, 33 seconds (2019).

GLOSSARY

acclimatize—to adjust or get used to a new environment

alpine—relating to higher mountain elevations

altitude sickness—swelling of the lungs or brain caused by air pressure at high altitudes

crampon—a metal plate with spikes attached to a boot for walking or climbing on rock or ice

crevasse—a deep crack in a glacier or other body of ice

ethnic—of or relating to a large group of people connected by common racial, national, tribal, religious, linguistic, or cultural origin

lichen—an organism made up of fungus and algae growing in partnership

novice—having the ability of a beginner

saddle—a ridge connecting two peaks

Seven Summits—a group that includes the tallest mountain on each of the seven continents

SELECTED BIBLIOGRAPHY

BBC. "Kabardino-Balkaria Profile." August 28, 2023. https://www.bbc.com/news/world-europe-20594299.

De Waal, Thomas. *The Caucasus: An Introduction*. New York: Oxford University Press, 2019.

Griffin, Nicholas. *Caucasus: A Journey to the Land between Christianity and Islam*. Chicago: University of Chicago Press, 2004.

Reynolds, Maura. "Ice Queen Demands Respect at Each Step." *Los Angeles Times*. August 4, 2001. https://www.latimes.com/archives/la-xpm-2001-aug-04-mn-30466-story.html.

Saikaly, Elia. "Mt. Elbrus—Off to Climb Europe's Highest Peak." August 15, 2012. https://eliasaikaly.com/mt-elbrus-off-to-climb-europes-highest-peak.

Schaeffer, David N. *Five Big Mountains: A Regular Guy's Guide to Climbing Orizaba, Elbrus, Kilimanjaro, Aconcagua, and Vinson*. Macon, Ga.: Mercer University Press: 2010.

Sinelschikova, Yekaterina. "Why Do So Many Die on Elbrus, the Bane of White-Collar Novices?" Russia Beyond. October 8, 2021. https://www.rbth.com/lifestyle/334283-die-elbrus-highest-mountain.

WEBSITES

7 Summits Club
https://7summitsclub.com
Learn about the world's tallest peaks and the people who climb them.

Mount Elbrus
https://armchairmountaineer.com/mt-elbrus
Explore Elbrus's geography, wildlife, and routes to its peak.

Prielbrusye National Park
https://national-parks.org/russia/prielbrusye
Discover the natural wonders surrounding Mount Elbrus.

INDEX